BENCHMARK BIOGRAPHIES

Heroic Sioux Warrior
CRAZY HORSE

by Virginia Schomp

BENCHMARK BOOKS

MARSHALL CAVENDISH
NEW YORK

In memory of my first hero—my dad, Russell F. Schomp

Benchmark Books
Marshall Cavendish Corporation, 99 White Plains Road, Tarrytown, New York 10591-9001

Library of Congress Cataloging-in-Publication Data
Schomp, Virginia, date.
Heroic Sioux warrior: Crazy Horse / Virginia Schomp.
p.   cm. — (Benchmark biographies) Includes bibliographical references and index.
Summary: A biography of the Oglala leader who steadfastly resisted the white man's attempt to take over Indian lands.
ISBN 0-7614-0522-4 (library binding)
1. Crazy Horse, ca. 1842–1877—Juvenile literature. 2. Oglala Indians—Biography—Juvenile literature. [1. Crazy Horse, ca. 1842–1877.
2. Oglala Indians—Biography. 3. Indians of North America—Biography.] I. Title. II. Series.
E99.O3C7292   1998   978'.0049752'0092—dc21   [B]   96-39121   CIP   AC

Printed in Hong Kong

Front cover: In *Fort Laramie* by A. J. Miller, a Sioux band camps outside the army fort
Back cover: Work progresses at the Crazy Horse Memorial, in the Black Hills of South Dakota.

Photo research by Richard Schomp

Photo Credits : Front cover: Detail, The Walters Art Gallery, Baltimore; back cover: Rob DeWall; page 4: Joslyn Art Museum, Omaha, Nebraska/Gift of the Enron Art Foundation; page 7 (top): The Bettmann Archive/Darley, artist; page 7 (bottom): Little Bighorn Battlefield National Monument; pages 9, 13, 31, 32: North Wind Picture Archives; pages 10, 21 (top): North Wind Picture Archives/Frederic Remington, artist; page 15: The Bettmann Archive/George Catlin, artist; pages 16, 38: State Historical Society of North Dakota; pages 18, 22: Stock Montage; page 21 (bottom): Wyoming Division of Cultural Resources; page 25: Courtesy of the James D. Horan Western Americana Collection/Charles Schreyvogel, artist; page 26: South Dakota State Historical Society/State Archives; page 28: Nebraska State Historical Society; page 29: Reproduced from *A Pictographic History of the Oglala Sioux*, by Amos Bad Heart Bull, text by Helen H. Blish, by permission of the University of Nebraska Press/© 1967 by the University of Nebraska Press/© renewed 1995 by the University of Nebraska Press; pages 33, 34: Courtesy Sid Richardson Collection of Western Art, Fort Worth, Texas/Herbert M. Herget, artist, Oscar E. Berninghaus, artist, respectively; page 37: Library of Congress; page 40: *A Pictographic History of the Oglala Sioux*, Amos Bad Heart Bull, University of Nebraska Press; page 42: The National Cowboy Hall of Fame and Western Heritage Center, Oklahoma City, Oklahoma/Frederic Remington, artist.

CONTENTS

A Boy Called Curly   5

"A Great Name"   12

The Sioux War   19

"The Life of a Warrior"   27

"Strong Hearts, Brave Hearts"   36

Glossary   43

To Learn More About Crazy Horse and the Sioux   45

Index   47

The Sioux Indians lived in tepees covered with buffalo hides. They moved their villages often in search of fresh hunting grounds and grass for their ponies.

A BOY CALLED CURLY

A DISTURBANCE IN CAMP

Smoke from the evening cookfires twisted above the Sioux (SUE) Indian camp. In the August heat, women stirred their soup pots. Men dozed or sat talking, puffing on wooden pipes. Some squatted beside the dusty trail the whites had carved through Indian country.

A line of covered wagons creaked along the trail. Behind the wagon train walked a white man with a scrawny cow. Suddenly the cow bolted. It charged the camp, trampling tepees and food boxes.

Dogs barked. Children shouted. A warrior ended the disturbance by shooting the cow with an arrow.

The animal's owner was furious. He hurried to nearby Fort Laramie. With cannons gleaming, thirty blue-coated soldiers rode to the Sioux camp. Chief Conquering Bear tried to make peace, offering five strong ponies for the dead cow. But the soldiers lost patience. Their mighty guns roared. Conquering Bear collapsed in a pool of blood. Then a wave of warriors rushed the bluecoats, war clubs waving and arrows flying. In minutes all the soldiers lay dead.

The Sioux wanted no more trouble. Quickly they packed up their ponies and set out for their northern hunting grounds. On the long journey, six warriors carried Conquering Bear in a buffalo hide sling. One boy caught a glimpse of the dying chief. Curly felt sickened and confused by all that had happened. Reaching the north country, the young Sioux hopped on his pony and headed for the hills alone.

THE TRAIL TO WAR

In the early 1800s, many thousands of Indians lived on the American Great Plains. Like an ocean of tall grasses, the Plains stretched north and south clear across the middle of the country.

There were many tribes of Plains Indians—Cheyenne (SHY-ann), Arapaho (ah-RAH-puh-hoh), Comanche (kah-MAN-chee), Crow. The largest and most powerful tribe was the Sioux.

The heart of Sioux life was the buffalo. Huge herds of the big shaggy beasts roamed the Plains. Riding bareback on fast ponies, Sioux hunters charged into the herds, shooting arrows and dodging the sharp horns. One good hunt in the fall provided enough meat to last a long hard winter. From the buffalo's hide came clothing and tepee covers, from its bones tools and weapons—every part of the animal was put to good use.

In the 1840s, white pioneers began crossing the Plains. Their wagon trains scared off the buffalo. Bound for new settlements out west, the travelers stuck

Young hunters risked their lives for the honor of killing the largest or the most buffalo.

To give thanks for a good hunt, villagers painted the finest hide and spread it out on a hilltop.

to a dusty road called the Oregon Trail. Their cattle ate up the grass along the trail, and their axes chopped down the cottonwood trees. The whites brought new diseases, too. Whole Indian villages sickened and died.

Angry warriors began stopping the wagons, demanding payments of coffee, sugar, and other treats. Sometimes they stole a rifle or a stray horse or cow. Then the whites built forts along the trail. They called a meeting of all the Plains tribes. At this great council, the whites offered to give each tribe a wagon train full of presents every year for fifty years. In return, the Indians must agree to leave the pioneers alone.

The headmen of the tribes signed the friendship treaty. The peace would last three years, until 1854. That was the year an argument over a runaway cow led to the first battle of a long war between whites and Sioux.

CURLY'S VISION

Curly was about twelve years old when he rode into the hills as Conquering Bear lay dying. The boy's nickname came from his curly brown hair. A Sioux boy did not get his real name until he earned it by performing some important deed.

Curly's hair and his pale skin set him apart from other Sioux boys, with their black braids and reddish brown coloring. Curly was different in other ways, too. He was daring and skillful but quiet and shy. By age eleven, he had ridden a wild horse and killed his first buffalo, but he never bragged about his brave deeds as other boys did.

Through blazing heat and bitter cold, a constant stream of white people pushed westward on the Oregon Trail.

When he was ten years old, Curly proved his bravery by catching and taming a wild Plains horse.

Now, in his quiet way, Curly had decided it was time for his vision quest. All teenage boys made this sacred journey, camping alone and waiting for a vision, or dream. The dream showed a boy the path he would take as a man. Warrior or holy man, horse catcher or healer—wherever his dream pointed, the boy must follow.

Riding to a hilltop, Curly stretched out on the gravel. He placed sharp stones between his toes to keep himself awake. For two days and nights, he waited, without eating or drinking. Just when he was ready to give up, his vision came. He saw a brown-haired man floating above the ground on horseback. On the man's cheek was a lightning bolt, on his chest hailstones. Arrows and bullets flew all around the vision man and his own people grabbed his arms, but he shook them off and rode on unharmed. Then the people closed in, shouting and grabbing, as a hawk cried overhead.

Curly woke to find his father shaking him. The boy returned home, carrying his vision in his heart. It would be three years before he told anyone about the dream that had shown his future as a great warrior and leader of his people.

"A GREAT NAME"

The mighty Sioux nation was made up of many tribes. The tribes of the western Plains were called the Lakota (lah-KOH-tah) Sioux. Curly's parents came from Lakota tribes—his father from the Oglalas (ahg-LAH-lahs), his mother from the Brulés (broo-LAYS). A year after Conquering Bear's death, the boy was camped with a small band of Brulés near the Oregon Trail.

It had been a good year, rich in buffalo. Curly had become a fine hunter. He had gone on his first horse-stealing raid against an enemy tribe. And along with his Brulé friends, he had pestered the pioneers whose wagons were ruining good hunting grounds. Surrounding the wagon trains, the boys scared the whites into giving them guns and bullets, coffee and crackers.

One afternoon, Curly returned from a hunting trip. Dark smoke lay like a blanket over the Brulé camp. Tepees, robes, food boxes—everything had been burned. Following a jumbled trail of footprints, the boy saw the bodies of

Sioux men, women, and children.

Stooping, Curly was sick to his stomach. Then anger washed through him like a cold wind. All that long night, he followed the fleeing people's trail. In the darkness, he found one woman hiding, the body of a tiny baby in her arms. Gently the boy placed the woman on a stretcher so his pony could pull her to safety.

In the morning, Curly caught up with the escaping Brulés. The people told their terrible story. Six hundred soldiers had surprised the peaceful village. The army had killed eighty-six people and taken seventy prisoners in revenge for the battle at Conquering Bear's camp.

Two weeks later, Curly's uncle Spotted Tail and two other Brulé warriors rode to Fort Laramie. The fort's commander had promised to end the war against the Sioux if the men gave themselves up. With their feet in iron chains, the warriors disappeared down the Oregon Trail. Watching, Curly swore never to surrender. It was better to die fighting.

GREAT LAKOTA COUNCIL

The tepees formed a giant circle on the northern mountain Bear Butte (BYOOT).

Five thousand Lakota from seven tribes had gathered to talk about the whites.

While the headmen met in the council lodge, Curly visited family and friends. It had been more than a year since he had seen his parents, sister, and brother. Also among the Oglalas were his friends He Dog and Hump. Among the Miniconjou (min-i-KAHN-joo) Sioux was his seven-foot-tall cousin Touch the Clouds. As Curly laughed with these friends, his eyes often turned to the pretty Oglala girl Black Buffalo Woman.

Along with the visiting and laughter, there was much serious talk at the council. In the east, the whites were forcing Indians onto fenced-in reservations. In the south, they had taken over the lands along the Oregon Trail. Many Sioux feared their own warriors were no

After the attack on the Brulé village, thousands of Sioux gathered for a council at the ancient meeting place Bear Butte.

match for the blue-coated soldiers. Even Spotted Tail, the brave Brulé who had spent a year locked up in a white prison, had come home saying it was useless to fight.

Now, seeing their great numbers, the Sioux found new hope. Surely such a strong nation could not easily be defeated. As the council ended, the chiefs agreed to fight together to defend their lands and people.

VISION OF POWER

Leaving Bear Butte, Curly and his father rode to a hilltop over the valley where

Curly's uncle, Spotted Tail, was a brave warrior who made peace with the whites to try to save his people.

Curly had been born. The boy was fifteen now, almost a man. It was time to talk about the vision that had come as Conquering Bear lay dying.

Curly's father listened quietly. Then the wise man helped his son understand his dream. The brown-haired man was Curly himself. The boy must always dress for battle as his vision man had dressed. He must ride first in the fighting and never take anything for himself. If he did these things, no enemy bullet or arrow could ever harm him. This was a vision of great power. And never before had the people been so in need of a powerful leader.

A BRAVE DEED

An unknown tribe had been spotted on the western Plains. Curly rode with the Oglala war party sent to challenge them. Carefully he prepared himself like the man in his vision. He placed a hawk's feather in his hair, painted his face with a lightning bolt, and dotted his chest with hailstones.

It was a hard battle. For two hours, the enemy hid in a sheltered spot on a hill and fired with many rifles. Suddenly Curly charged straight toward them, riding untouched through a wall of bullets. He killed one man with an arrow, leaped his horse over the body, and quickly shot a second warrior.

That night the village celebrated the return of the warriors and the many fine ponies they had captured. As the people cheered, each young man sang about his deeds. Twice Curly was pushed into the circle around the campfire. Twice the quiet young warrior backed out. In the end, it was Curly's father who proudly sang a song for his brave son:

> *My son has been against the people of unknown tongue.*
> *He has done a brave thing;*
> *For this I give him a new name, the name of his father,*
> *and of many fathers before him—*
> *I give him a great name*
> *I call him Crazy Horse.*

Curly's father called out his brave son's new name.

THE SIOUX WAR

Around the Powder River, in the northwestern Great Plains, lay the finest hunting grounds in America. In 1858, the Lakota left the ruined southern Plains and headed for that rich region. They fought many battles with the Crow and Shoshone (shoh-SHOH-nee) tribes for control of the Powder River country. In those battles, no warrior fought with more skill or daring than Crazy Horse.

Thinner and shorter than most men, Crazy Horse was not especially fierce looking when he dressed for battle in his simple breechcloth and hawk's feather. Yet other warriors were quick to join up when Crazy Horse led a raiding party. They knew that the brave Sioux always hit what he aimed at and never left behind a wounded friend. They also knew he gave away every pony he captured.

By age twenty-one, Crazy Horse was feared and respected throughout the Plains. But fame could not win the one thing he wanted most. For years he had been in love with Black Buffalo Woman, niece of the Oglala chief, Red Cloud. Often he felt the girl's shy brown eyes watching him, too. But he was the son of a simple holy man, and Red Cloud wanted his niece to marry into a powerful family. One day, Crazy Horse returned from battle to find that Black Buffalo Woman had married No Water, the brother of a tribal leader.

More troubles followed. From the southern Plains came word that soldiers had attacked a village of friendly Cheyenne. More than one hundred women and children had been killed. Among them was Crazy Horse's friend Yellow Woman, the young mother he had pulled to safety after the attack on the Brulé camp.

Cheyenne riders crossed the Plains with a war pipe. Thousands of Oglalas, Brulés, and Arapahoes answered the call. The huge party of warriors swept across the south like wildfire. They attacked and burned ranches, wagon trains, and stagecoach stations, killing every white person they found. Even chiefs who had argued for peace with the whites joined the fighting. The time for talk was over. This was a war to the finish.

A SPOILED PLAN

Crazy Horse led twenty men toward the Platte Bridge, where the Oregon Trail crossed the North Platte River. The whites had built Fort Casper to protect the bridge. The Sioux and Cheyenne planned to destroy the fort, cutting the trail in two.

Drawing near the bridge, Crazy Horse

Indian warriors attacking wagon trains skillfully dodged the pioneers' bullets by riding on the side of their ponies.

Fort Casper and the bridge across the North Platte River

In the Sioux attack on Fort Casper, Crazy Horse acted as a decoy, drawing the enemy out toward a force of hidden warriors.

waved his buffalo blanket. Whooping and shouting, he and his men pretended they were trying to capture the horses on the other side. Soldiers rushed from the fort. The Sioux warriors dashed off, bullets whistling around their feet. Rolling out their cannon, the soldiers followed. Crazy Horse's party cried out as if afraid, whipping their ponies with one hand, secretly holding them back with the other.

Over the next hill, three thousand war-painted warriors waited. Crazy Horse led the soldiers closer and closer to the trap. But before the army reached the foot of the hill, the impatient young warriors burst from hiding. One look up at a skyful of Indians and the soldiers scrambled back to their fort.

The headmen were furious. Too many times, the young warriors had spoiled a plan with their impatience. In battles against other Indian tribes, they were used to fighting independently. Each tried to outdo the others, to prove himself the bravest and best. But that kind of fighting didn't work against the whites. The soldiers fought together, as one strong united team. The Indians must learn to do the same or they would never win.

SHIRT OF HONOR

Maybe unity could be found in an old Sioux custom. In years past, the tribe's strongest young warriors had been chosen to become shirt-wearers, men who headed all the other warriors, keeping peace and order among them. They watched over the poor and helpless and worked for the good of all the people.

Now, as crowds cheered, horsemen rode through the village, calling out the names of three sons of chiefs. The cheering was loudest when the people heard the name of the fourth shirt-wearer, Crazy Horse.

POWDER RIVER BATTLES

Over the next three years, the Lakota battled fiercely to protect their hunting grounds. A new trail to the western gold fields had been carved right through the Powder River country. Guarding the Bozeman Trail was Fort Phil Kearny. At the fort, Captain William Fetterman bragged that with eighty men, he could conquer the whole Sioux nation.

One cold December morning, a small war party attacked soldiers gathering wood a few miles from the fort. Fetterman marched to the woodcutters' rescue with a force of eighty men. Pretending to lead a wounded pony, Crazy Horse tricked Fetterman into following him five miles, to where two thousand Indians were hiding. This time the warriors waited for their signal. Hooves thundered and arrows rained. All the soldiers were killed.

Farther north on the Bozeman Trail, the Cheyenne attacked Fort C. F. Smith. To the south, the Sioux raided Fort Reno. All along the trail, warriors attacked soldiers and travelers. Not a single wagon train passed unharmed.

By 1868, the whites were tired of fighting. The soldiers marched away from the Bozeman Trail forts, and the Indians burned them to the ground. In a

To save their Powder River hunting grounds, the Sioux attacked forts all along the Bozeman Trail. "Crazy Horse always led his men himself when they went into battle," said He Dog, "and he kept well in front of them."

council at Fort Laramie, Chief Red Cloud signed an agreement ending the Sioux War. The treaty promised that the whites would stay out of the Powder River country forever.

Chief Red Cloud, who planned the Powder River battles that saved the Sioux hunting grounds . . . for a while

"THE LIFE OF A WARRIOR"

After the Sioux War, Red Cloud traveled to Washington to meet President Ulysses S. Grant. The Oglala chief had never seen such tall buildings and massive cannons. Awed by the whites' power, he agreed to move his people south to a reservation.

Crazy Horse refused to give up his freedom. With about five thousand other Sioux, he remained in the Powder River country. There he led many successful war parties against the Shoshone and Crow. Often his friend He Dog fought by his side. One summer, as the two returned from a raid, the village came out to honor them. The warriors were presented with the two sacred lances of the Oglalas. "These spears were each three or four hundred years old," He Dog said later, "and were given . . . to those in the younger generation who had best lived the life of a warrior."

When not fighting or hunting, Crazy Horse spent much of his time visiting the tepee of Black Buffalo Woman. One day, the two rode from camp together. Black

He Dog, Crazy Horse's lifelong friend

Buffalo Woman had decided to leave No Water and marry Crazy Horse. An Oglala woman had the right to leave her husband, and he was expected to accept her choice. But No Water had a jealous temper. Grabbing a pistol, he followed the lovers. He burst into their tepee and shot Crazy Horse in the face.

It was many days before Crazy Horse's wounds healed. By then, No Water had escaped to the Red Cloud reservation, taking Black Buffalo Woman with him. With a blackness in his heart, Crazy Horse returned his shirt of honor to the tribe's elders. He had broken his promise to keep peace among the people. He could no longer be a shirt-wearer.

A WIFE AND DAUGHTER

Crazy Horse had lost the woman he

The Sioux kept records of important happenings through picture writing, or pictographs. He Dog's nephew Amos Bad Heart Bull drew this pictograph of warriors carrying sacred lances.

loved and the respect of his people. Hump, his best friend, had died fighting the Shoshone. Little Hawk, his brother, was killed by white miners. How could one man stand so many losses?

He Dog worried about his silent, lonely friend. He arranged a marriage with the quiet Oglala woman Black Shawl. With a new wife and then a baby daughter, Crazy Horse felt the pain in his heart easing. His bow again brought meat to poor villagers' cooking pots. And when he rode out to battle, the people sang a song to honor their strongest warrior.

RETURN OF THE SOLDIERS

An old enemy was back to test the strength of all the warriors. Four years after the last soldiers left the Powder River country, a party of white surveyors appeared in the north. Guarded by four hundred bluecoats, the surveyors were marking a path for the railroad. To fight these invaders, Crazy Horse joined forces with the leader of the northern Hunkpapa Sioux, Sitting Bull.

The warriors attacked the soldiers' camp. For hours, bullets flew from one side, arrows from the other. The two Lakota leaders worked hard to outshoot the enemy and just as hard to impress each other. First Crazy Horse rode his pony slowly past the line of blazing rifles. Then Sitting Bull strolled toward the soldiers, sat down just out of reach of their bullets, and calmly began puffing on his pipe.

Soon after that daring stunt, the surveyors packed up and headed home. Next year they would return, protected

The railroad brought even more whites to the Powder River country.
Between 1830 and 1850, they wiped out twenty-five million buffalo.

by an army commanded by Lieutenant Colonel George Armstrong Custer.

"LONG HAIR" CUSTER

The Cheyenne hated the yellow-haired officer they called "Long Hair." In 1868, Custer and his men had sneaked up on a sleeping Cheyenne village and killed one hundred people. Five years later, Crazy Horse got his first look at the famous soldier and Indian fighter. When Custer's Seventh Cavalry crossed the northern Plains to protect the returning railroad surveyors, Crazy Horse and Sitting Bull attacked. The two sides fought a number of small battles, with no real winner.

George Armstrong Custer led his Seventh Cavalry in many battles with the Plains tribes.

Custer's army marched into the Black Hills of South Dakota. To the Sioux, these mountains were sacred, the home of Wakan Tanka, their Great Spirit. The peace treaty signed at Fort Laramie had promised that the whites would stay out of the Black Hills forever. But when Custer sent reports of "gold among the grass roots," miners swarmed to the holy mountains.

At first, Crazy Horse ignored the invaders. He had suffered another terrible loss and could think of nothing else. His beloved daughter, They Are Afraid of Her, had died from the white man's disease cholera (KAH-luh-ruh).

Crazy Horse named his daughter They Are Afraid of Her, saying, "She shall grow up a great mother of the people."

When Custer found gold in the Black Hills, miners rushed to the Sioux's sacred mountains.
The Indians called the miners' trail the "Thieves' Road."

For three days, Crazy Horse lay with the child's small body on a death platform on the prairie. When he returned home, he spoke little. When he fought again, he was fiercer and more daring than ever.

A ycar after They Are Afraid of Her's death, runners brought a message from the Red Cloud reservation. The whites were calling the Sioux to a council. They wanted to talk about buying the Black Hills. Crazy Horse sent his own message: "One does not sell the earth upon which the people walk." Then orders came from the white government. All Sioux must move south to the reservations. Crazy Horse answered by taking his people north to join Sitting Bull's camp. Soon the northern Plains filled with the tepees of ten thousand Indians preparing for one last big fight in defense of their lands.

"STRONG HEARTS, BRAVE HEARTS"

The huge camp on the northern Plains rang with songs and laughter. At the promise of a good fight, thousands of Sioux had left the reservations. Now old friends clasped hands, families visited and feasted, and children raced their ponies.

In all the fun, the villagers almost seemed to forget the dark cloud hanging over them. Sitting Bull and Crazy Horse remembered. In June 1876, they held an ancient religious ceremony, the Sun Dance, to strengthen the people's ties to the Great Spirit. For eighteen hours, Sitting Bull danced around the sacred Sun Dance pole. Then he had a vision: he saw many soldiers falling defeated into the Lakota camp.

Three days later, Cheyenne scouts came galloping. One thousand bluecoats were marching north, under General George "Three Stars" Crook. Crazy Horse led fifteen hundred warriors to meet them. By Rosebud Creek, the Indians attacked. They charged again and again, using lances and war clubs to knock the

Sioux warriors attack Crook's cavalry in the Battle of the Rosebud. "This is a good day to die!" Crazy Horse cried as he led a charge straight into the soldiers' guns.

Chief Sitting Bull

soldiers off their horses. The whites, with twice as many rifles, forced the warriors back. But Crazy Horse helped turn the retreat around, until it was the soldiers who were running.

After six hours, the Indians scattered and the soldiers headed south. Three Stars' army had been stunned by the new way the warriors were fighting. They had charged as one powerful, united force. One soldier later said that he "never saw so many Indians at one time before . . . or so brave."

BATTLE OF THE LITTLE BIGHORN

"Long Hair" Custer was back. A few days after the Battle of the Rosebud, scouts brought word that the Seventh Cavalry was marching toward the Indians' new camp, in the valley of the Little

Bighorn River. What the scouts didn't know was that Custer had divided his army of 611 men into three groups. He planned to hit the village on two sides at once, with the third group waiting across the river to cut off the Indians' escape.

Custer's men took their positions. Suddenly they opened fire on the southern end of the camp. The villagers were taken by surprise. Quickly the warriors grabbed their weapons. Just as quickly, they turned the soldiers' attack into a retreat. Shooting arrows and swinging war clubs, the warriors forced the bluecoats to scramble back across the river.

Crazy Horse rode up as the shooting died down. "Strong hearts, brave hearts, to the front!" he cried. Turning his pony, he dashed toward the camp's northern end, where Long Hair was leading the second group of soldiers.

CUSTER'S LAST STAND

Custer's attack had turned into a fight for life. Battling hundreds of Sioux warriors, he and his men were backing step by step up a tall hill. If the soldiers could make it to the top, their quick-firing rifles would hold off the warriors until help arrived. But just before they reached their goal, a single man appeared above them. Crazy Horse had circled around the hill and climbed the opposite side. Behind him glistened the spears and arrows of one thousand warriors.

With a fierce battle cry, the Indians swept down the hillside. Custer and his men fought bravely, but in twenty minutes the Battle of the Little Bighorn was over. Not a soldier was left standing.

Crazy Horse (top center) *rides with his warriors at the Battle of the Little Bighorn.*
This pictograph was made by Amos Bad Heart Bull.

SURRENDER

Winter came, and the huge camp on the northern Plains split up. Crazy Horse led his followers back to their Powder River hunting grounds. The snow was deep and the winds bitter cold. The buffalo were gone. Ponies died, and the hungry people ate them. Huge new armies prowled the Plains, with orders to kill every Indian living outside the reservations. In the middle of that hard winter came the hardest news of all. The whites had forced the reservation chiefs to sign a treaty giving up the Powder River country and the Black Hills.

On his own, Crazy Horse would have fought forever. But the good of the people must come first. Many were sick, and all were starving. The warriors were tired, and there were too few to stand up to an attack.

In May 1877, a line of nine hundred Oglalas and two thousand ponies paraded into Fort Robinson, Nebraska. All the officers crowded around to watch the surrender of the famous Sioux leader Crazy Horse. "Three Stars" Crook promised Crazy Horse his own reservation in the Powder River country. But some of the Lakota headmen grew jealous of all the attention the thirty-six-year-old warrior was getting. They whispered that the wild Sioux was planning to go on the warpath again. Crook heard the rumors and gave orders for Crazy Horse's arrest.

On the way to jail, just in sight of a tiny windowless cell, Crazy Horse made a break for freedom. One of his own people grabbed his arms—just as he had seen in his childhood vision. Then a

No picture was ever taken of Crazy Horse, but his friend Short Bull said the heroic warrior was "not like the rest of us . . . . He had black eyes that hardly ever looked straight at a man, but they didn't miss much that was going on."

soldier stabbed the helpless warrior with a bayonet. Crazy Horse was carried to an officer's room. An hour later, with his father and his cousin Touch the Clouds near, he died. Touch the Clouds went outside to tell the waiting people.

"It is well," the tall warrior said quietly. "He has looked for death, and it has come."

*   *   *

Today about fifty thousand Sioux live on reservations in North and South Dakota. In the Black Hills, a colossal sculpture slowly takes shape. When it is finished, the figure of Crazy Horse, carved out of an entire mountain, will loom as tall as a sixty-story skyscraper. The spirit of this great American hero will again watch over the lands he fought so hard to save for his people.

Glossary

breechcloth: A strip of cloth held up by a belt around the waist, worn by Indian men.

council: A meeting held so people can discuss a problem and make plans to solve it.

holy man: A wise adviser to tribal leaders, who had the special ability to understand the meaning of dreams.

Lakota: The seven tribes—Oglala, Brulé, Miniconjou, Hunkpapa, Sans Arc, Two Kettle, and Blackfoot—of the western branch of the Sioux nation.

Oregon Trail: The trail across the Great Plains used by white settlers traveling to the American West in the mid-1800s.

reservation: Lands set aside by the United States government for Native Americans.

retreat: An escape from battle, made by the losing side.

shirt-wearer: A Sioux leader who was responsible for keeping peace among the people of the tribe and protecting the poor and helpless.

Sun Dance: An ancient religious ceremony of the Plains Indians, performed to renew the people's ties with the sacred spirits.

treaty: An agreement between two governments.

vision quest: A ceremony performed by all Sioux boys, in which the boy camped alone in a holy place and waited for a dream that would show the work he must do as an adult.

wagon train: A line of covered wagons traveling together.

Wakan Tanka: The Sioux's Great Spirit, the sacred force present in all living things.

To Learn More About Crazy Horse and the Sioux

Books on Crazy Horse

Hook, Jason. *Crazy Horse: Sacred Warrior of the Sioux.* Poole, Dorset, U.K.: Firebird Books, 1989. (Distributed in the United States by Sterling Publishing Company, New York.)

St. George, Judith. *Crazy Horse.* New York: G. P. Putnam's Sons, 1994.

Sanford, William R. *Crazy Horse: Sioux Warrior.* Springfield, NJ: Enslow Publishers, 1994.

Wheeler, Jill C. *The Light-Haired One: The Story of Crazy Horse.* Bloomington, MN: Abdo & Daughters, 1989.

Books on the Sioux

Crow, Moses N. *Hoksila and the Red Buffalo.* Chamberlain, SD: Tipi Press, 1991. [Retells an ancient Lakota legend about a young warrior.]

Flood, Renee S., editor. *A Legend from Crazy Horse Clan.* Chamberlain, SD: Tipi Press, 1987. [Retells an ancient Lakota legend about a young girl and a baby raccoon.]

Henckel, Mark. *Battle of the Little Bighorn.* Helena, MT: Falcon Press, 1992.

Sneve, Virginia D. *The Sioux: A First Americans Book.* New York: Holiday House, 1993.

Videos

America's Great Indian Leaders. 1995. Media Process Group, Questar Video, 680 North Lake Shore Drive, Suite 900, Chicago, IL. 60611. [Examines the lives of four native Americans who fought to protect their people: Geronimo, Quanah Parker, Chief Joseph, and Crazy Horse.]

Crazy Horse: The Last Warrior. 1993. A & E Home Video, P.O. Box 2284, South Burlington, VT 05407.

Places to Visit

Crazy Horse Memorial: If you travel to South Dakota, you'll want to visit the awe-inspiring Crazy Horse Memorial, which is being carved out of Thunderbird Mountain, seventeen miles from Mount Rushmore. The Indian Museum of North America, on the same site, is a good place to learn about Sioux life in Crazy Horse's times. The phone number is 605-673-4681.

Little Bighorn Battlefield National Monument: In southeast Montana, near the town of Hardin, you can relive the Battle of the Little Bighorn at the Little Bighorn Battlefield National Monument, two miles southeast of the Crow Agency Indian Reservation. The phone number is 406-638-2621.

Fort Walsh National Historic Site: In the Canadian province of Saskatchewan, you can tour the visitors' center and old-time trading post at the Fort Walsh National Historic Site. There you'll learn about the years Sitting Bull and his people spent in Canada after the Battle of the Little Bighorn. Fort Walsh is part of the Cypress Hills Interprovincial Park, near Maple Creek. The phone number is 306-662-2645.

Index

Page numbers for illustrations are in boldface

Amos Bad Heart Bull, **29**, **40**
appearance, of Crazy Horse, 8,
19, **42**

Battle of the Little Bighorn, 38-
39, **40**
Battle of the Rosebud, 36-38, **37**
battles
    Crazy Horse in, 17, 20-23, **22**,
    25
    for Powder River country, 19
    techniques in, **21**, **22**
Black Buffalo Woman, 14, 19-
20, 27-28
Black Hills, 33, **34**, 35, 41
Black Shawl (wife), 30
Bozeman Trail, 24-26
bravery, of Crazy Horse, 17-18,
19, **25**
buffalo, 6, **7**, 31

Cheyenne, 20-23, 24, 32
Conquering Bear, Chief, 5-6
Crazy Horse, **40**

Crazy Horse Memorial, 42
Crook, General George, 36-38,
41
Curly (Crazy Horse's early
name), 6
vision of, 8-11, 17
Custer, Lieutenant Colonel
George Armstrong, **32**, 32-
33
at the Little Bighorn, 38-39

death, of Crazy Horse, 41-42
decoy, Crazy Horse as, **22**, 23, 24
diseases, from pioneers, 8, 33

father, Crazy Horse's, 16-18, **18**,
42
Fetterman, William, 24
Fort Casper, 20-23, **21**, **22**

Great Lakota Council, 14-16, **15**

He Dog, 14, 25, 27, **28**, 30
horses, **10**, **21**

hunting. *See also* buffalo
    by Crazy Horse, 8, 12, 30

land
    whites taking, 14
leaders, 17, 23-24, 41
    Crazy Horse as, 19, **22**, **25**, 38

miners, in Black Hills, 33, **34**

names, Sioux, 8, 18
No Water, 20, 27-28

Oregon Trail, 6-8, **9**, 14, 20-23

pictographs, **29**, **40**
pioneers. *See* wagon trains
Powder River country, 30-32, 41
    battles for, 19, 24-26

railroads, 30-32, **31**
Red Cloud, Chief, 20, **26**, 27
reservations, Sioux, 14, 27, 35,
36, 42

shirt-wearers, 23-24, 28
Sioux, **4**, 6, 12
    and soldiers, 12-14, **13**, 20-26
    Council of, 14-16
    reservations for, 35, 36
Sitting Bull, Chief, 30-32, 35, 36,
    38
soldiers, 5-6, 30
    attacks on Indians by, 12-14,
        13, 20, 32
    forts of, 20-23, 24-26

Spotted Tail (uncle), 14, **16**
starvation, of Indians, 41
Sun Dance, 36
surrenders, 14, 41

teamwork, 23, 38
tepees, Sioux, **4**
They Are Afraid of Her (daugh-
    ter), 30, **33**, 33-35
Touch the Clouds (cousin), 14, 42
treaties, 8, 26, 33, 41

visions, 36
    of Crazy Horse, 8-11, 17,
        41-42

wagon trains, **9**, 24
    and Sioux, 5, 6-8, 12
warriors, Sioux, 23, 27, **29**
weapons, 36-38, 39
whites, 14. *See also* soldiers;
    wagon trains

ABOUT THE AUTHOR

"When I was growing up, I thought American history started with the Pilgrims landing at Plymouth Rock. Today there are so many more good books and movies about the Americans who were here *before* the Pilgrims. Learning about Native American history—and about the lives of heroes like Crazy Horse—gives us a better, truer understanding of our country's past."

Virginia Schomp is the author of the Benchmark Biography *He Fought for Freedom: Frederick Douglass* and of many other books for young readers, on topics including states, countries, history, and animals. Ms. Schomp lives in Monticello, New York, with her husband, Richard, and their son, Chip.